P9-DWS-448

MEDIEVAL MAYHEM

TIMOTHY KNAPMAN

QEB

QEB Publishing

Cover Design: Punch Bowl Design
Illustrator: Andrea Da Rold
Editor: Amanda Askew
Designer: Andrew Crowson

QED Project Editor: Ruth Symons
Managing Editor: Victoria Garrard
Design Manager: Anna Lubecka

First published in the United States in 2013 by
QEB Publishing, Inc.
3 Wrigley, Suite A
Irvine, CA 92618

www.qed-publishing.co.uk

A CIP record for this book is available from the Library of Congress.

ISBN 978 1 60992 487 4

Printed in China

Photo credits
Shutterstock: BVO, 33; Antonio Abrignani, 36; Jorisvo, 38;
istock: Linda Steward, 27

How to begin your adventure

Are you ready for an amazing adventure in which you must face deadly foes, survive terrible dangers, and solve fiendish puzzles? Then you've come to the right place!

Medieval Mayhem isn't an ordinary book—you don't read the pages in order, 1, 2, 3.... Instead you jump forward and backward through the book as you face a series of challenges. Sometimes you may lose your way, but the story will always guide you back to where you need to be.

The story begins on page 4, where there are questions to answer and puzzles to solve. Choose which answer you think is correct. For example:

 IF YOU THINK THE CORRECT ANSWER IS A, GO TO PAGE 37

 IF YOU THINK THE CORRECT ANSWER IS B, GO TO PAGE 13

If you think the correct answer is A, turn to page 37 and look for the same symbol in blue. That's where you will find the next part of the story.

If you make the wrong choice, the text will explain where you went wrong and let you have another chance.

The problems in this book are about life in the Middle Ages. To solve them, you must use your historical knowledge, as well as common sense. To help you, there's a glossary of useful words at the back of the book, starting on page 44.

Are you ready?
Turn the page and let your adventure begin!

WELCOME TO THE
MIDDLE AGES

You are the King's best knight and it is your job to keep him safe. It's no easy task because there are many who would like the King dead so that they can take his place!

IF YOU'RE UP TO THE CHALLENGE, **STRIDE BOLDLY** TO PAGE 23

No, a cauldron is a large metal pot for cooking over an open fire. Witches were thought to brew potions in them.

GO BACK
TO PAGE 20
AND TRY AGAIN

 Correct! Monks live in a monastery.

You ride as fast as you can to the monastery. The abbot, the most important monk, greets you and you tell him about your quest.

I will give you what you seek, if you can prove that you are a man of learning. What language is spoken during religious services?

LATIN.
TURN TO
PAGE 12

GREEK.
CHECK ON
PAGE 31

That's right! They are known as a "coat of arms." Heralds make sure that two knights never use the same colors and symbols.

The crowd cheers as you thunder toward your opponent. You need to knock him off his horse. Miss! Two more attempts to go. . . . You try again—and he nearly hits you! Last try. . . . You hit him in the chest so hard that your lance shatters. But he stays on his horse!

The crowd goes wild and chants, *"Round two, round two, round two!"*

"But what is the next round?" asks your squire.

What do you say?

YOU KEEP JOUSTING UNTIL ONE OF YOU IS KNOCKED OFF. **CHECK ON** PAGE 18

YOU KEEP JOUSTING UNTIL ONE OF YOU IS DEAD. **GO TO** PAGE 26

YOU FIGHT ON FOOT. **TURN TO** PAGE 39

 No, smallpox caused pimples and blisters.

GO BACK
TO PAGE 41
AND TRY AGAIN

GO BACK **TO PAGE 41** **AND TRY AGAIN**

  No, this is a jester. He tells stories, juggles, and performs acrobatics.

GO BACK **TO PAGE 25** **AND PICK AGAIN**

 Knights don't wear different colored armor.

TURN BACK **TO PAGE 42** **AND HAVE ANOTHER TRY**

 A battle-ax is a big weapon, heavy to lift and difficult to swing in a small space. You'll be cut to pieces before you get a chance to attack.

GO BACK TO PAGE 40 **AND CHOOSE AGAIN**

You give the King the antidote, and within minutes his face returns to its usual color. You have saved his life! You then tell the King what you have learned.

CANNON.
GO TO
PAGE 18

ONAGER.
TURN TO
PAGE 28

TREBUCHET.
HEAD TO
PAGE 14

> We will punish Baron Roderick for what he has done. His castle is well defended, so we must be prepared with the best siege weapons. What should we take?

Your archers might miss the enemy and hit your own men— they're too close!

FLIP BACK TO PAGE 16 AND THINK AGAIN

No, you haven't done anything to earn a medal yet.

GO BACK TO PAGE 39 AND CHOOSE AGAIN

Yes, you win your opponent's armor! Baron Roderick storms back to the castle, grumbling that he's never liked Saturdays. You hope that he calms down before the great feast tonight.

Before the feast begins, you go to the kitchens to check the King's food. The King has many enemies who would love to poison him on his birthday.

Something's not right.
Which food shouldn't be here?

FOUR AND TWENTY BLACKBIRDS, BAKED IN A PIE. GO TO PAGE 20

PIKE FISH IN AN ONION AND CINNAMON SAUCE. TURN TO PAGE 16

ROASTED BOAR WITH APPLE SAUCE. HEAD TO PAGE 28

That's him—a minstrel is a musician. You chase after him, but he escapes.

The King is taken to his bedchamber. You follow to see how you can help. The King's physician arrives.

> I need to remove the poison. Fetch the draining remedy from the table.

What do you give him?

A JAR OF LEECHES.
GO TO PAGE 43

A BOTTLE OF WINE.
TURN TO PAGE 13

A TREPANNING KNIFE.
HEAD TO PAGE 19

A MANDRAKE.
FLIP TO PAGE 38

The longbow is a powerful weapon that has won many battles, but it's no use in close-combat fighting.

TURN BACK
TO PAGE 40
AND PICK
ANOTHER WEAPON

Correct! Latin was the universal language of the Catholic Church. The Bible was translated into Latin and all church services were conducted in Latin.

In our monastery, we look after the bones of a dead saint. Some people travel many miles to see them and pray to the saint. What are such people called?

TOURISTS?
GO TO PAGE 21

PILGRIMS?
TURN TO PAGE 32

FRIARS?
CHECK ON PAGE 27

The lance and spear would be useless in close combat. These are weapons to use on horseback.

GO BACK
TO PAGE 39
AND THINK AGAIN

 Wine was used to clean wounds, but not to remove poison.

TURN BACK
TO PAGE 11
AND TRY AGAIN

No, Merlin was the great King's friend and wizard.

GO BACK
TO PAGE 17
AND HAVE
ANOTHER TRY

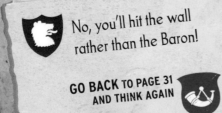 No, you'll hit the wall rather than the Baron!

GO BACK TO PAGE 31
AND THINK AGAIN

Correct! The trebuchet will hurl huge rocks at the castle walls, breaking them down.

You lead an army to Baron Roderick's castle. The King was right. The castle is well defended and the Baron refuses to surrender.

We must capture the keep!

Which part of the castle is that?

THE STONE FORTRESS. **FIND OUT** ON PAGE 26

THE HILL-LIKE MOUND IN THE MIDDLE OF THE CASTLE. **TURN TO** PAGE 39

THE AREA WHERE THE SERVANTS LIVE. **LOOK IT UP** ON PAGE 20

THE DITCH FILLED WITH WATER. **CHECK** ON PAGE 30

Pike was a very popular dish in the Middle Ages, and was often served with this thick sauce.

GO BACK TO PAGE 10 AND THINK AGAIN

At seven years old, you became a page—an apprentice squire. You served a knight and only became a squire when he thought you were good enough.

GO BACK TO PAGE 19 AND TRY AGAIN

You order the men to charge at the heavy wooden doors of the keep with a battering ram.

Baron Roderick's archers fire arrows. Other men throw stones and pour hot water down on you from openings in the walls called "murder holes." Is there any way to protect your men?

TELL YOUR OWN ARCHERS TO FIRE ON THEM. **TURN TO** PAGE 10

COVER YOUR MEN WITH A SIEGE MACHINE. **FLIP TO** PAGE 40

RETREAT. **TURN TO** PAGE 19

Correct. Peasants work the land to provide food for everyone.

You knock on the door and an old woman answers. You explain that you are the King's knight and you've come to ask her for help.

Before I let you in, I must make sure you are really a knight by asking you some questions. . .
Question One: What was the name of the great king of legend whose knights sat at a round table?

LANCELOT?
GO TO PAGE 26

MERLIN?
TURN TO PAGE 13

ARTHUR?
FIND OUT ON PAGE 39

No, you had three attempts to knock Geoffrey off his horse. Now you must face a new challenge to win the tournament. **GO BACK TO PAGE 7 AND HAVE ANOTHER TRY**

 That's right! At one time, a knight was also struck on the back of the neck with a sword. Ouch!

And finally, what is the code that all knights must live by?

THE CODE OF CHIVALRY. TURN TO PAGE 27

THE CODE OF THE KING. GO TO PAGE 36

 In the Middle Ages, cannon were slow to load, and the balls were difficult to aim at an exact target.

GO BACK TO PAGE 9 AND CHOOSE SOMETHING ELSE

No, a trepanning knife was used to cut a hole in the skull. It was thought to let evil out of a mad person's head.

TURN BACK TO PAGE 11 AND TRY AGAIN

Retreat is not an option—the King wants you to defeat Baron Roderick!

TURN BACK TO PAGE 16 AND CHOOSE ANOTHER ANSWER

A palfrey is the horse for you—it's fast and will give you a smooth ride over a long distance. Your squire chooses a rouncy for himself. He saddles up both horses and you head out at once.

After many hours riding, you stop for a rest.

Sir, I hope I become a knight, just like you. How old were you when you became a knight?

What is your answer?

21 YEARS OLD. GO TO PAGE 20

14 YEARS OLD. TURN TO PAGE 33

SEVEN YEARS OLD. HEAD TO PAGE 16

The pie wouldn't taste nice, but it is not there to be eaten. When it's cut open, the blackbirds fly out—an entertaining spectacle for the King and his guests.

 No, this part of the castle is called the bailey.

FLIP BACK TO PAGE 15 AND THINK AGAIN

GO BACK TO PAGE 10 AND TRY A DIFFERENT ANSWER

 Yes, you became a full knight at 21 years old, after seven years of training.

At last, you reach the apothecary's town. You need to find the house—and quick! You ask a passer-by where it is.

"You don't want to go there. We think the apothecary practices witchcraft. People say she has a familiar. Do you know what that is?"

A CAT. **GO TO** PAGE 30

A BROOMSTICK. **HEAD TO** PAGE 37

A CAULDRON. **TURN TO** PAGE 5

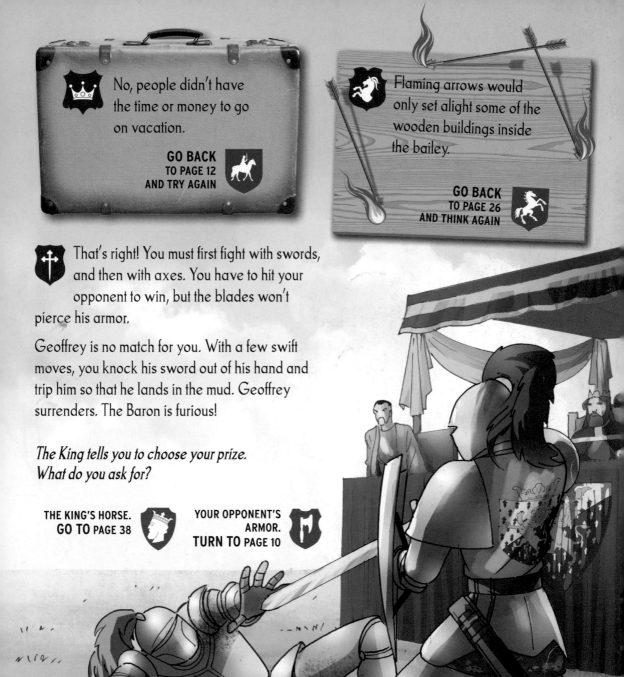

No, people didn't have the time or money to go on vacation.

GO BACK
TO PAGE 12
AND TRY AGAIN

Flaming arrows would only set alight some of the wooden buildings inside the bailey.

GO BACK
TO PAGE 26
AND THINK AGAIN

That's right! You must first fight with swords, and then with axes. You have to hit your opponent to win, but the blades won't pierce his armor.

Geoffrey is no match for you. With a few swift moves, you knock his sword out of his hand and trip him so that he lands in the mud. Geoffrey surrenders. The Baron is furious!

The King tells you to choose your prize. What do you ask for?

THE KING'S HORSE.
GO TO PAGE 38

YOUR OPPONENT'S ARMOR.
TURN TO PAGE 10

Correct! It was the law that farmers had to give a tenth (a "tithe") of what they grew to the Church as a sort of tax, and this food was stored in a special barn.

Your squire fetches food and water for you both. You meet him at the stables.

Which horse do you choose for a long journey?

A DESTRIER?
GO TO
PAGE 41

A ROUNCY?
TURN TO
PAGE 28

A PALFREY?
CHECK ON
PAGE 19

Today is Saturday, the King's birthday. The guest of honor is Baron Roderick, a cunning and powerful man. He controls a large army, which is vital to the King. But you suspect he may have his eye on the throne . . .

The King is holding a jousting tournament. You will battle Baron Roderick's best jouster, Sir Geoffrey.

First, you need to dress for the tournament. Your squire, a young boy who serves you, is new and is still learning.

No, nuns live in a nunnery.

GO BACK
TO PAGE 29
AND TRY AGAIN

No, that's too dangerous —there are archers at the top, waiting to fire down at you.

GO BACK
TO PAGE 37
AND THINK AGAIN

Which armor would you like for the tournament, sir?

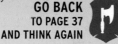

SUIT A.
TURN TO
PAGE 38

SUIT B.
CHECK ON
PAGE 42

SUIT C.
FLIP TO
PAGE 31

23

The page serves the King's food and the celebration is a success. After everyone has eaten, the entertainment begins. There are musicians, dancers, and jugglers everywhere.

Suddenly, the Queen screams. The King's face is bright red and he is clutching his throat!

"The King has been poisoned! It was the minstrel! Seize him!" the Queen orders.

You draw your sword —but which figure is the minstrel?

FIGURE 1.
FIND THE ANSWER
ON PAGE 30

FIGURE 2.
CHECK ON PAGE 8

FIGURE 3.
TURN TO PAGE 11

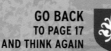

No, Lancelot was a great knight, but not a king.

GO BACK
TO PAGE 17
AND THINK AGAIN

Tournaments can be fatal, but they are meant to be contests, and certainly not fights to the death.

GO BACK
TO PAGE 7
AND TRY AGAIN

You're right! The keep is the most secure part of the castle. You'll need to plan well if you're going to take it.

The trebuchet hurls rocks at the outside walls, but they are too strong to be breached.

The King says it's time for undermining. What does he want you to do?

DIG TUNNELS UNDER THE WALLS AND SET EXPLOSIVES INSIDE THEM. **FLIP TO** PAGE 37

WAIT FOR BARON RODERICK'S FOOD TO RUN OUT. **CHECK ON** PAGE 42

FIRE FLAMING ARROWS INTO THE CASTLE. **TURN TO** PAGE 21

Yes, the code of chivalry. The code said that knights needed to be brave and honorable on the battlefield, and to treat enemies fairly.

The apothecary trusts you.

You tell her the King's symptoms and at once she starts to prepare a cure.

Friars were religious men who traveled around the country, but they didn't go only to look at bones.

GO BACK TO PAGE 12 AND TRY AGAIN

But one ingredient is missing— an herb that you can only find with the holy men who live over yonder. The priest in the next village will take you there. Find him, but hurry!

YOU SEND YOUR SQUIRE BACK TO THE CASTLE WITH THE NEWS AND CONTINUE TO THE NEXT VILLAGE ON PAGE 41

27

The onager—which is named after a kind of wild ass because it gives a powerful kick—could throw heavy rocks at the castle walls, but there are newer, and more deadly weapons you can choose.

TURN BACK
TO PAGE 9 AND CHOOSE AGAIN

  A rouncy is a good all-purpose horse, but it's only used by squires and poorer knights.

GO BACK TO
PAGE 22 AND PICK AGAIN

Correct—but not because it's dangerous. Today is Saturday and it is against Church law to eat meat on Wednesdays, Fridays, Saturdays, and throughout Lent and Advent—and even the King must obey.

You still need to check that the King's food isn't poisoned. You taste each dish in turn. Luckily they're all safe and you're still alive! Phew!

YOU'D BETTER GET READY FOR THE CELEBRATIONS ON PAGE 24

Correct! The sickness, or bubonic plague, is known as the Black Death.

"I must find him, no matter what!" you tell the woman.

"Then try the church," she says.

The church is easy to find. The door is ajar, so you go inside.

> Come no further!
> I have the sickness!

You tell the priest
why you have come.

> Take the map on the wall.
> Go to the monks and tell
> them I sent you.

*The map shows many buildings.
You don't have time to ride to them all.
Which one is the home of the monks?*

THE MONASTERY.
GO TO PAGE 5

THE NUNNERY.
CHECK ON
PAGE 23

THE CATHEDRAL.
TURN TO PAGE 36

Correct! Medieval people thought that witches kept cats, toads, and other small creatures because they believed evil spirits lurked in these animals' bodies.

You don't believe in witches, so you ask the boy to tell you where the apothecary lives.

 No, that's the moat. It's the castle's first line of defence.

GO BACK
TO PAGE 15
AND TRY AGAIN

 No, that's a page. He's there to bring food and drink to the King and his guests.

GO BACK
TO PAGE 25 AND
TRY AGAIN

The apothecary lives in a peasant's hovel on the edge of town. You know what a peasant is, don't you?

IT'S A POOR FARM WORKER. **GO TO PAGE 17**

IT'S A COOK. **TURN TO PAGE 42**

No, that's battle armor. It's more flexible for sword fighting, but it doesn't offer enough protection from your opponent's lance.

GO BACK
TO PAGE 23
AND PICK AGAIN

Greek was spoken in the Orthodox Church in the East, but not in the Catholic Church in the West.

TURN BACK TO PAGE 5 AND HAVE ANOTHER TRY

That's right—a short sword may not look like much, but it's what you want. It's easy to use quickly in a small space against many enemies.

You battle on, knocking down any soldiers in your path.

You storm down a spiral staircase—and there in front of you is Baron Roderick! He raises his sword to put up a fight.

Remember, you're above him on a spiral staircase— in which hand should you hold your sword to fight him?

LEFT. GO TO PAGE 13   **RIGHT.** TURN TO PAGE 34

That's right, they were pilgrims. It was believed that visiting holy places would earn you God's forgiveness for the bad things you did in your life.

The abbot shows you where to find the herb. You add it to the apothecary's mixture and ride like the wind for home.

You're nearly there when a beggar flags you down.

> I was the King's minstrel, but Baron Roderick told me to leave the castle at once or he'd lock me in a dungeon. One of his men took my place and poisoned the King!

RACE TO THE CASTLE TO SAVE THE KING AND TELL HIM THE TRUTH ON PAGE 9

The mace and war hammer are battle weapons and could kill your opponent, which you don't want to do.

GO BACK
TO PAGE 39
AND HAVE
ANOTHER TRY

 Not all knights wear a plume in their helmet for jousts.

GO BACK
TO PAGE 42
AND THINK AGAIN

 You had only just started training as a squire at 14 years old.

GO BACK TO
PAGE 19
AND TRY AGAIN

Correct! Spiral staircases in castles curved clockwise going up as a defensive measure. Weapons were normally held in the right hand, so if you're fighting downward, you can use yours more easily than the attacker coming up the stairs.

You hold Baron Roderick at the tip of your sword and march him to the King. He is put in chains and held by the King's guards.

"You are a brave knight. You have saved my life once again and captured the traitor. For this, I will make you a Lord and give you the Baron's land and riches. Congratulations!"

The food in a tithe barn isn't for animals.

GO BACK
TO PAGE 43
AND TRY AGAIN

Although the King lives by the code, it is not named after him.

GO BACK TO PAGE 18
AND TRY AGAIN

No, a cathedral is a large church where a bishop leads the worship.

GO BACK TO PAGE 29
AND HAVE ANOTHER TRY

A "familiar" is not a broomstick, though medieval people believed that witches flew through the night on broomsticks.

GO BACK TO PAGE 20 AND CHOOSE ANOTHER ANSWER

 Correct! But it's dangerous because the explosives are unstable....

All goes to plan and—BOOM! —you blow a huge hole in the wall from underneath. You lead the assault on the keep—but it has thick, stone walls and heavy wooden doors. The army waits for your word on what to do next.

What do you tell them?

USE A BATTERING RAM TO BREAK DOWN THE DOORS. GO TO PAGE 16

CLIMB THE WALLS. TURN TO PAGE 23

Although the King is pleased with you, asking for his horse would be rude.

GO BACK
TO PAGE 21
AND TRY AGAIN

 No, the mandrake root was thought to have magical powers—to stop pain and send patients to sleep.

GO BACK
TO PAGE 11
AND TRY AGAIN

 That's ceremonial armor. It looks good, but it's not meant to be worn in a fight and won't protect you.

GO BACK
TO PAGE 23
AND CHOOSE AGAIN

No, yellow fever causes fever, sickness, and muscle pain.

GO BACK
TO PAGE 41
AND TRY AGAIN

No, the huge hill-like mound in the middle is called the motte.

TURN BACK
TO PAGE 15
AND PICK
ANOTHER ANSWER

That's right! You'll have to take part in the next round: two fights on foot—each time with a different weapon. Which weapons do you choose?

**SWORD
AND AX.
TURN TO**
PAGE 21

 Correct! Arthur was the great King—but the apothecary has more questions.

"Question Two: When you were knighted, what did the ceremony involve?"

YOU WERE TAPPED
ON THE SHOULDER
WITH A SWORD.
TURN TO PAGE 18

**LANCE AND SPEAR.
HEAD TO** PAGE 13

YOU WERE
GIVEN A MEDAL.
HEAD TO PAGE 10

**MACE AND
WAR HAMMER.
GO TO** PAGE 33

Correct! The siege machine is called a "pentise" or "penthouse"—a wooden structure with a reinforced roof to deflect missiles. It is covered in wet animal hides so it can't be set alight.

Your men batter down the doors and pour into the keep. Baron Roderick's men are waiting for you. This is close-combat fighting, so which weapon do you choose?

A BATTLE-AX.
GO TO PAGE 8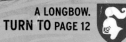

A LONGBOW.
TURN TO PAGE 12

A SHORT SWORD.
GO TO PAGE 31

No, the large and powerful destrier is a warhorse and it's not suited to a long journey at high speed.

GO BACK TO PAGE 22 AND CHOOSE AGAIN

The village is oddly quiet when you arrive.

You ask a passer-by where you can find the priest.

Stay away from the priest! He's covered in black, crusty swellings. He must have the plague. Do you know what else this disease is called?

SMALLPOX. GO TO PAGE 8

YELLOW FEVER. CHECK ON PAGE 38

BLACK DEATH. FIND OUT ON PAGE 29

No, a peasant isn't a cook.

GO BACK
TO PAGE 30
AND TRY AGAIN

 Starving the enemy out is a common tactic, but you'd have to wait a long time.

TURN BACK TO
PAGE 26 AND COME UP
WITH ANOTHER PLAN

Correct! This armor protects the chest and upper arms—the areas most likely to be struck by your opponent's lance.

You get dressed and head to the field. Your squire follows closely behind, carrying your lance. The crowd cheers as you arrive.

Sir, you're wearing a helmet. How does the crowd tell one knight from another?

What is your answer?

BY THE COLOR OF
YOUR HELMET'S
PLUME?
GO TO PAGE 33

BY THE COLOR OF
YOUR ARMOR?
TURN TO PAGE 8

BY THE SYMBOLS ON
YOUR SHIELD AND
ON THE COAT WORN
OVER YOUR ARMOR?
CHECK ON PAGE 6

Correct! In the Middle Ages, some people believed that illnesses were caused by an imbalance of "humors" (bodily fluids). They used leeches to suck a patient's blood—it was thought that this would make them strong again.

The apothecary lives a day's ride from here—you must hurry! Head due north until you reach the tithe barn, then turn east for 30 miles. Do you know what the tithe barn is?

You don't want to look stupid in front of the Queen, so answer quickly.

A BARN FOR STORING FOOD FOR ANIMALS. GO TO PAGE 36

A BARN FOR STORING FOOD GROWN FOR THE CHURCH. TURN TO PAGE 22

Glossary

Abbot
The most important monk, or holy man, at a monastery.

Apothecary
A person who made medicines from herbs and plants.

Armor
Clothing made out of metal that protected a knight's body during battle.

Battle-ax
A large ax used to give deadly blows in battle.

Black Death, or plague
A disease that spread across Europe in the 1300s, killing millions of people. It caused painful black swellings on the legs, neck, and armpits, as well as a fever, vomiting, and delirious behavior.

Cannon
A large gun that fired heavy metal balls.

Catholic Church
The organization that controlled how Christianity was practiced in western Europe in the Middle Ages. The church told everyone how to behave, and even what they could eat.

Coat of arms
A pattern or picture to identify a family. Knights wore coats of arms on their shields, banners, and coats over their armor so other knights could identify them in battle.

Code of Chivalry
A code that all knights followed. It said that knights should be brave and honorable on the battlefield, and treat enemies fairly.

Crossbow
A weapon that could shoot short, heavy arrows—called bolts—to cut through armor.

Destrier
A large, powerful horse that was used in battle.

Herald
A person who recorded the different coats of arms, so a pattern wasn't ever used more than once.

Jousting tournament
A contest between two knights on horseback, charging toward each other with long poles called lances. It was a way for knights to practice the arts of war and win glory when they had no battles to fight.

Keep
The strong fortress at the center of a castle. A king or lord often lived there.

Knight
A soldier who served a king or lord. He wore steel armor and fought in battle on horseback. A man trained for seven years before becoming a knight at 21 years old.

Latin
The language of the ancient Romans. It was adopted as the language of the Catholic Church, which was based in Rome.

Longbow
A weapon that was made of wood and shot arrows.

Mace
A weapon with a heavy spiked metal ball at the end of a short, wooden pole.

Middle Ages

A period of European history from about 1100 to 1500 CE.

Minstrel

A musician or singer in the Middle Ages.

Monk

A holy man who lives alone or with other monks in a monastery. The chief monk is called an abbot.

Monastery

A place where holy men called monks live.

Motte and bailey castle

An early type of castle where a circular wooden fortification was placed around a large mound of earth. The mound was called a motte, and the wooden fortification was called a bailey.

Onager

A type of catapult used to lay siege to a castle. It could throw heavy rocks at a castle's stone walls.

Page

A personal servant. A knight's page was a young boy who was learning to be a squire, but pages also worked in the households of powerful people.

Palfrey

A slim, muscular horse. It was fast and could travel long distances without tiring.

Pentise

A wooden structure with a strong roof to protect it against missiles. It was covered in wet animal hides so it couldn't be set alight.

Physician

A doctor. Doctors in the Middle Ages knew little about the human body, so many of their cures did more harm than good.

Rouncy

A small, strong horse that was mainly ridden by squires and poor knights.

Siege

When an army surrounded a defended building, such as a castle, so no one could get in with food or water. The soldiers inside would become weak, so the outside army could attack more easily.

Squire

A boy who was training to be a knight. He would serve a knight as a page for about seven years and, at around the age of 14, become a squire if the knight thought he was good enough. If he continued to work hard, he would become a knight around 21.

Trebuchet

A large weapon used to attack a castle. It was like a large catapult and hurled rocks at the castle walls.

Undermining

A siege technique whereby soldiers dug tunnels under the enemy's castle walls and set explosives inside them. This caused the walls to collapse so that the soldiers above ground could attack the castle.

Taking it further

The History Quest books are designed to inspire children to develop and apply their historical knowledge through compelling adventure stories. For each story, children must solve a series of historical problems on their way to completing an exciting quest.

The books do not follow a page-by-page order. The reader jumps forward and backward through the book according to the answers given to the problems. If their answers are correct, the reader progresses to the next part of the story; incorrect answers are fully explained before the reader is directed back to attempt the problem once again. Additional help may be found in the glossary at the back of the book.

To support the development of your child's historical knowledge, you can:

- Read the book with your child.

- Solve the initial problems and discover how the book works.

- Continue reading with your child until he or she is using the book confidently, following the "Go to" instructions to the next puzzle or explanation.

- Encourage your child to read on alone. Prompt your child to tell you how the story is developing, and what problems he or she has solved.

- Point out the differences and similarities between life in the Middle Ages and life today— what we wear, eat, and do for fun.

- Discuss what it would be like if someone from the Middle Ages visited us today. Or if we went back in time to a great castle.

- Take advantage of the many sources of historical information —libraries, museums, and documentaries. The Internet is another valuable resource, and there is plenty of material specially aimed at children. Take care only to visit websites endorsed by respected educational authorities, such as museums and universities.

- Remember, we learn most when we're enjoying ourselves, so make history fun!